Healing Creations

PATRICIA FITZGERALD studied Visual Education & Communication, Philosophy & Sociology, and is qualified in the Therapeutic Use of Mindfulness. Discovering mandalas at a time of personal upheaval utterly changed her life. She practises mindfulness daily, and exhibits and hosts workshops and retreats in Ireland and abroad. For more information, visit Patricia's website: www.healingcreations.ie.

You can also keep up-to-date at:

 facebook.com/healingcreationsbymandalaflame

 twitter.com/healingcre8ions

 instagram.com/healingcreations

The beauty of Patricia Fitzgerald's mandalas was a pleasure for me as a reader. Colouring the mandalas is a calming and meditative act of creation for those who are fortunate enough to own a copy of this book. Set in the mindfulness tradition, her book provides a deep and enduring antidote to the stresses of our age.

Padraig O'Morain, author of *Mindfulness for Worriers* and other books

With Healing Creations, *Patricia Fitzgerald does what all great healers aspire to do – she has found a way that people can relax, feel entertained, and simultaneously profoundly change the way their internal chemistry and personal story have been playing out. Her effective solution to very complex wounds and life disappointments is the meditative practice of colouring in mandalas – deceptively simple. This ancient wisdom meets its modern form in Patricia's innovative work. I highly recommend this book as a way of affecting life changes for the better.*

Judymay Murphy, International Motivational Speaker

For Rebecca

Her angel's face,
As the great eye of heaven shined bright,
And made a sunshine in the shady place.

EDMUND SPENSER

Healing Creations

PATRICIA FITZGERALD

The Collins Press

HALO

Birds perch to rest at the heart as if to listen intently;
Beady eye ready for the strum of spinning circles;
A drum to keep time with it all.
That they might fly and never fall inside a perfect circle.

A nucleus, a hush of planetary wonder lust
Electric cosmic dust echoing what has been spiraling for centuries.
Indian intricacies overlap with Celtic whisperings,
As Buddhist mantras kneel in chakra balancing.

To ease a silver fish into the stream of flowing knots.
Dot follows dot to play a picking up of forgetmenot paths.
Ask the way back and mark the spot for the eye to dive,
into the belly of a black ocean.

A bubbling, a reckoning, storm in a teacup
Gilded, fired up, spinning crackling then somehow fluttering.
Dripping, glistening, tears crystallised in a mastery;
An asking please for holy healing alchemy.

These windows we witness, echoing a symphony of glowing dreams.
Halos harnessed, winking through the darkness
for all who see to pause and breathe
and dare to dream of peace.

ALICE MCCULLOUGH

Introduction

THINK OF THIS BOOK AS BUBBLE BATH FOR YOUR SOUL. A way for you to relax and take care of your inner spirit. We take it for granted to care for our physical bodies, our homes and the things external to us. The nature of life brings many journeys, both good and bad. We move from childhood to adulthood, negotiating the educational system of our country, which may or may not be for us. We are then required to make a decision on what it is we want to do in life. Some of us are sure, most of us not so sure. We feel pigeonholed into whatever it is we choose for life. This doesn't have to be the case. We have the potential and the capacity to be many things. Then there are relationships, and our expectations of Hollywood romance. We go through love, break-ups, marriages, divorces, pregnancy, child rearing, IVF, financial abundance, financial ruin, birth and death, sickness and health. In a nutshell, we have good times and we have bad times. It is natural.

Each journey, whether we perceive it as positive or as negative, brings about an uneasiness in us. Change happens all the time. And dealing with change can be worrisome. The best journey of my life was when I was pregnant with my daughter. Beautiful though it was and excited as I was, I often found times when I worried so much that I would not be a good mother, that something terrible would happen ... movies that would play out in my mind in bed at night. (By the way, thank goodness, none of them became reality!) Some years later there came a not-so-nice journey. I divorced, and that too brought much stress and worry, but somehow became the most precious learning experience that I have ever known. It was during this time that I began to draw mandalas. I wasn't quite sure as to what they were or the historical and spiritual significance of them. The only thing that I knew was that they made me feel extraordinarily calm. That worrying was futile. That I could control only what I could control. The rest I had to trust. They brought about self-awareness, connection and peace of mind.

Can colouring a mandala really help you deal with stress and change? Yes! The act of creating and engaging with an intuitive piece of art brings you into a place of calmness, where negativity can be released and where decisions can be made in a much more focused manner. It brings about a quiet mind, where you can become aware of the ways in which you speak to yourself. Are you berating yourself because you went outside the line, or got a colour wrong? You will find that this small-scale thinking between you and your mandala will mirror the way you speak to yourself or feel about the larger issues in your life. Becoming aware is the first step. When you find yourself doing this, ask yourself: 'Would I speak to a good friend this way?' If the answer is no, well, why are you speaking to yourself in that way? Through this process you can become your own best friend.

I do not mean for you to repress negative emotions or feelings, but to become aware of them. Accept the bad times as you accept the good times. The way you speak to yourself can help you in both circumstances. It is about being compassionate to yourself. How can you be compassionate to another if you cannot be so to yourself?

This book contains forty hand-drawn mandalas for you to engage with, all intuitively created. You also have journal pages to write down your thoughts and feelings as they arise during or after the process. Be aware of your body when you feel an emotion. Identify the emotion and accept it, good or bad. Really take a good look at it. Where in your body do you feel it? What colour would you give it if it were to have a colour? What shape? What texture would it be? Acknowledging how we truly feel, rather than how we think we should feel, is a really important element of any mindfulness practice. And understanding that it is perfectly okay to feel that emotion. Allow yourself to feel that emotion without judgement.

You can use this book as a regular activity or to document a particular life journey, be that a pregnancy (there are forty mandalas and forty weeks in pregnancy – what a nice, calming way to connect with your baby and yourself), a house move, an engagement, travelling, treatment for an illness or a journey of grieving.

When colouring the mandala, use whatever colour feels right for you. Don't let your mind tell you 'well, that blue doesn't go with that orange' or 'that wouldn't match the curtains in the sitting room'. Let the patterns jump out at you, and trust your intuition. Add patterns and shapes as you wish. Ignore shapes if you wish. Add your own shapes. Use whatever materials feel right for you. They don't have to be expensive. Use markers, paint, crayons or colouring pencils. Metallic pens are great for adding extra detail over colours. Play. Have fun. Let go. Allow yourself to be. Both in the colouring and in the writing.

Permit yourself to trust in the experience. By letting go of having a particular outcome in mind and instead trusting the intuitive process, all kinds of unforeseen possibilities can emerge. You will find as you go through this practice, your thoughts become clearer. Perhaps there has been a problem spinning around in your head, a decision that you can't make. Maybe something some-body said to you today is niggling at you, or a look somebody gave you. Perhaps you have been ill and are feeling down. Or you are a nervous flyer about to board an aircraft. Whatever your situation, balancing the mind in this creative way clears the path for a solution and calmness to emerge.

There is a science to this. Psychologists, neurologists and researchers have found that by stimulating both sides of the brain (which mandala art is doing) our thought process becomes clearer, stress reduces, blood pressure lowers and the list goes on. Normally when we make decisions or review our day we use the left hemisphere of the brain, considered as rational. We often leave out the possibility of taking advantage of the benefits brought by the brain's right hemisphere, such as creative imagination and serenity. By working intuitively within the wholeness of the circle, we begin to get a much fuller picture of what is going on in our lives and our minds.

I have been creating mandalas almost every day now for four years. Just focusing those thoughts, getting rid of what is not mine. It is a form of open-eyed meditation and works wonders on spring-cleaning the soul. It is fascinating to look back on the pieces and journalled thoughts to see how far you have come, the patterns that emerge, the inevitable ups and downs of life. So when you are feeling down, you can look back and see how you dealt with it last time, and see that it passed and that you came out the other side and can again.

The colouring of mandalas might seem like a small thing to do. But small changes lead to big shifts.

The History and Meaning of Mandalas

Mandalas are a very ancient art form and can be found right across the world. The name itself comes from the ancient Sanskrit word for 'circle', or 'container of spirit'. Mandalas are usually symmetrical geometric designs enclosed within a circle, a square or a rectangle. They have traditionally been used as focal points for meditation. From Hinduism and Tantric Buddhism, ancient Chinese and Japanese culture, to Celtic traditions and Indo-European culture, mandala designs can be found in abundance.

Although the forms and functions can differ, they have many attributes in common, for example, a central starting point (often referred to as the 'Bindu'), geometric design, symmetry and the philosophical idea that the mandala represents our oneness with the universe. The universe itself is fundamentally composed of geometric forms and movement that harmoniously express an underlying divine structure. From the macroscopic to the microscopic world, geometric patterns and movement are prolific. Look at the way the planets move so perfectly around the sun. The way our galaxies swirl in spirals. How our moon orbits the earth. How we can see via satellite imagery the swirling, spiralling nature of cloud formations and storms. Then, moving closer, we can see the way birds dance in spiralling flocks or murmurations, the beauty and geometric nature of each and every flower. Cut open any fruit to see the stunning geometry contained within. Think of pinecones and snowflakes. Our very own eyes are mandalas – the windows to our souls. And then close in even further to inside our bodies. Have you ever see cells under a microscope? Each nucleus is the Bindu of a mandala in each and every cell, spiralling around each other in perfect synchronisation.

And now bring to mind the cyclical patterns in our lives: the seasons come and go as sure as day and night come and go. Birth and death. Youth and age. The perfect balance of male and female on our planet. Imagine, the natural sex ratio of the human species is 100:101, which is pretty astounding. Think of the tide, in and out, pulled by the moon. Just like your breath, in and out, with absolutely no effort from you. It is a wonderful world that we inhabit, with perfect balance and symmetry in all things. Mandalas can bring us back to the wonderment of all that we are and all that surrounds us. That we do not operate alone, but move in patterns within patterns. For you to have bought this book means that someone had to create it, another to publish it, the technology had to be invented to do all of this. The delivery person who brought the book to the shop, the people working in the shop, the builders of the shop, the creator of your art materials … and on it goes! The interrelatedness of humanity is quite astounding and I feel sure that if it could be viewed from the outside, it would appear as beautiful and seamless as a dancing murmuration of starlings. Mandalas can help us see the bigger picture and pattern of our own immediate lives and relationships, and then further and further afield.

When you are working with your mandala, you are engaging with these universal archetypal patterns of oneness. It is a thoroughly enjoyable experience to engage in merely for the sake of it. For your own peace and pleasure. When coloured for the purposes of healing, mandalas can alleviate anxiety, tension and boredom, helping you to become serene, calming your mental activity. When coloured for spiritual exploration, they will bring about a consciousness of the universal oneness of all things.

The Meaning of Colour

Across time and place, colour holds meanings for us. These meanings can vary hugely from culture to culture. For example, black in one culture will denote grief or mourning, whereas in another culture, that colour would be white. You will also have your own personal associations to colour, which are equally correct for you. For the purposes of this book, I will look at the colours associated with our seven major chakras, or energy centres in the body often associated with the endocrine system. You are drawn to the colours you need most in life. Colours influence our mood and emotions. They impact on our sense of ease or unease.

THE SEVEN CHAKRAS

Crown Chakra: Sahasrara
Spirituality/Connection to a
Higher power

Third Eye Chakra: Ajna
Intuition
Foresight

Throat Chakra: Vishuddha
Communication
Speaking your truth

Heart Chakra: Anahata
Love for Self
Love for others
Unconditional Love

Solar Plexus Chakra: Manipura
Confidence
Self-Esteem

Sacral Chakra: Swadhisthana
Creativity
Sexuality

Root Chakra: Muladhara
Security
Connection to earth/roots

First Chakra: *Muladhara*: Red

The first chakra, also known as the base or root chakra, is located at the end of the spine. The colour associated with this chakra is red. It symbolises our connection to the earth, our sense of place. When we look at a tree, we know that its roots penetrate deeply into the earth, holding it securely. We, too, have a root system that secures us in place. Security comes in many forms: the food we eat, the shelter we have, financial security. Having a healthy root system is vital. Fear can undermine this energy centre, for example, fears about safety, security, trust and lack. Red is the colour of life force. It is the colour of our blood. The energy of red is a dominant one. It demands our attention. It is authoritative and can denote ambition. It can also be associated with anger. That anger will usually have root in feelings of insecurity or lack.

Second Chakra: *Swadhisthana*: Orange

Often referred to as the sacral chakra, this energy centre is located just below the navel. Orange is a very sensual colour and this chakra is related to our feelings of sacredness. It is the location of the energy for our creativity and sexuality. Our pleasure centre. A healthy second chakra will ensure good appetite, curiosity, compassion, vitality and aliveness. An unhealthy sacral chakra can mean rigidity, poor boundaries and social skills.

Third Chakra: *Manipura*: Yellow

The third chakra, also called the solar plexus chakra, is represented by the colour yellow. The ancient Sanskrit word literally translates to 'city of jewels'. It is located in the middle of the abdomen and it is here that we generally sense our 'gut feelings'. Containing almost as many nerve endings as the brain, it is often referred to as the second brain. It is our centre of intuition and the seat of our emotions. It is here that we feel excitement or fear, butterflies in the stomach. Associated with the sun, this chakra holds a vital energy of confidence and exuberance. When it is healthy, we will be confident, cheerful and energetic. When unhealthy, we will be unsure, listless and feeling down.

Fourth Chakra: *Anahata*: Green

Located in the heart, this energy centre is that of love. Love for others and love for the self. In order to have a healthy heart chakra, all past issues must be healed and forgiveness reached. Self-love is key here. How you love yourself, you love others. How you forgive yourself, you forgive others. A weak heart chakra can give rise to hatred, jealousy, envy and mistrust. A healthy heart chakra affords love, affection, kindness, confidence, self-worth and respect. The word Anahata literally means unhurt.

Fifth Chakra: *Vishuddha*: Blue

Vishuddha, or the throat chakra, is located in the throat. This chakra is all about authentic self-expression and speaking your truth. It is about becoming who you really are without fear of what others might say or think. Not speaking the truth may block this chakra. It is not only about you speaking your truth, but also about allowing others to do the same and to really listen with compassion and acceptance.

Sixth Chakra: *Ajna*: Indigo

Referred to as the Third Eye, this chakra point is located just above the centre point of the two eyebrows. It is the seat of intuition or our sixth sense and imagination. It represents that inner knowing or perception that we all possess. An unhealthy Ajna chakra may mean that you are lacking in insight and may have trouble concentrating.

Seventh Chakra: *Sahasrara*: Violet or white

Located at the top of the crown, Sahasrara, or the crown chakra, is the seat of connection to something bigger than ourselves. It is our gateway to our higher selves. It is our point of connection to wisdom and to being at one with the world. When it is healthy, we are inspired, connected, self-aware and spiritually enriched. When unhealthy, we may feel unimaginative, disconnected and alone.

Notice the colours that you are drawn to and really take a look at why. Hold awareness of how you are feeling during the process of colouring and of writing. Acknowledge and accept it without judgement. Relax and be free with your creativity and allow yourself to simply be. And most of all, have fun along the way! If you would like to share your finished pieces or thoughts with me, please feel free to post to my Facebook page:
www.facebook.com/healingcreationsbymandalaflame

Namaste
PATRICIA FITZGERALD

MEDITATION

Notice the room or location where you are right now. Bring awareness to your breath. Notice what you see. Notice the smells. The textures. The sounds. Now try to notice something, using each sense, that you haven't noticed before.

JOURNAL

Pervading Emotion

....

....

....

Where in your body do you feel it?

....

....

....

Colour of Emotion

....

....

....

Shape of Emotion

....

....

....

Texture of Emotion

....

....

....

By bringing a calm awareness to the changing moments,
we bring a calm awareness to our changing lives.

Padraig O'Morain, *Mindfulness for Worriers*

JOURNAL

JOURNAL

JOURNAL

Pervading Emotion

....

....

....

Where in your body do you feel it?

....

....

....

Colour of Emotion

....

....

....

Shape of Emotion

....

....

....

Texture of Emotion

....

....

....

Trust yourself. Create the kind of self that you will be happy to live with all your life. Make the most of yourself by fanning the tiny inner sparks of possibility into flames of achievement.

Golda Meir

JOURNAL

JOURNAL

JOURNAL

Pervading Emotion

....

....

....

Where in your body do you feel it?

....

....

....

Colour of Emotion

....

....

....

Shape of Emotion

....

....

....

Texture of Emotion

....

....

....

If you don't like something, change it.
If you can't change it, change your attitude.

Maya Angelou

JOURNAL

JOURNAL

JOURNAL

Pervading Emotion

....

....

....

Where in your body do you feel it?

....

....

....

Colour of Emotion

....

....

....

Shape of Emotion

....

....

....

Texture of Emotion

....

....

....

Whether you believe you can do a thing or not, you are right.

Henry Ford

JOURNAL

....

....

....

....

....

....

....

....

....

....

....

....

....

....

....

....

....

....

JOURNAL

MEDITATION

Gaze at the mandala. Bring awareness to your breath without changing it. Notice how your breath feels cooler on inhalation and warmer on the exhalation. Realise that your breath happens with no effort from you. Just like the tide.

JOURNAL

Pervading Emotion

....

....

....

Where in your body do you feel it?

....

....

....

Colour of Emotion

....

....

....

Shape of Emotion

....

....

....

Texture of Emotion

....

....

....

Sometimes the fastest way to start doing what works for you
is to simply stop doing what doesn't work.

Jeffrey Allen

JOURNAL

JOURNAL

JOURNAL

Pervading Emotion

....

....

....

Where in your body do you feel it?

....

....

....

Colour of Emotion

....

....

....

Shape of Emotion

....

....

....

Texture of Emotion

....

....

....

No one can make you feel inferior without your consent.

Eleanor Roosevelt

JOURNAL

JOURNAL

....

....

....

....

....

....

....

....

....

....

....

....

....

....

....

....

....

JOURNAL

Pervading Emotion

....

....

....

Where in your body do you feel it?

....

....

....

Colour of Emotion

....

....

....

Shape of Emotion

....

....

....

Texture of Emotion

....

....

....

*Your dream is not some far distant land, it is a method, a way
of showing up daily that results in the ultimate outcome.*

Judymay Murphy

JOURNAL

....

....

....

....

....

....

....

....

....

....

....

....

....

....

....

....

....

....

JOURNAL

JOURNAL

Pervading Emotion

....

....

....

Where in your body do you feel it?

....

....

....

Colour of Emotion

....

....

....

Shape of Emotion

....

....

....

Texture of Emotion

....

....

....

And remember, no matter where you go, there you are.

Confucius

JOURNAL

JOURNAL

....

....

....

....

....

....

....

....

....

....

....

....

....

....

....

....

....

....

MEDITATION

Gaze at the mandala. Bring awareness to your breath. Become aware of your body. Try to bring your awareness to, and feel your presence in, each and every part of your physical body.

JOURNAL

Pervading Emotion

....

....

....

Where in your body do you feel it?

....

....

....

Colour of Emotion

....

....

....

Shape of Emotion

....

....

....

Texture of Emotion

....

....

....

Wherever there is a human being,
there is an opportunity for a kindness.

Seneca

JOURNAL

JOURNAL

JOURNAL

Pervading Emotion

....

....

....

Where in your body do you feel it?

....

....

....

Colour of Emotion

....

....

....

Shape of Emotion

....

....

....

Texture of Emotion

....

....

....

When your heart speaks, take good notes.

Judith Campbell

JOURNAL

JOURNAL

JOURNAL

Pervading Emotion

....

....

....

Where in your body do you feel it?

....

....

....

Colour of Emotion

....

....

....

Shape of Emotion

....

....

....

Texture of Emotion

....

....

....

Tomorrow is always fresh, with no mistakes in it yet.

L. M. Montgomery, *Anne of Green Gables*

JOURNAL

....

....

....

....

....

....

....

....

....

....

....

....

....

....

....

....

....

....

JOURNAL

JOURNAL

Pervading Emotion

....

....

....

Where in your body do you feel it?

....

....

....

Colour of Emotion

....

....

....

Shape of Emotion

....

....

....

Texture of Emotion

....

....

....

*You don't have to work five days a week miserably earning
the right to live the remaining two days as you wish.
All seven days belong to you and you can live them
in productive and legendary style.*

Judymay Murphy

JOURNAL

....

....

....

....

....

....

....

....

....

....

....

....

....

....

....

....

....

....

JOURNAL

MEDITATION

When working on colouring your next mandala, bring awareness to how tightly you hold the pen and how hard you lean on the page. The pen will work no matter how tightly or loosely you hold it.

JOURNAL

Pervading Emotion

....

....

....

Where in your body do you feel it?

....

....

....

Colour of Emotion

....

....

....

Shape of Emotion

....

....

....

Texture of Emotion

....

....

....

Now and then listen to the chatter in your mind without getting caught up in it. You may be surprised at the extent to which the mind pointlessly re-runs the same old comments, memories and judgements, especially those that make you feel bad.

Padraig O'Morain, *Mindfulness on the Go*

JOURNAL

JOURNAL

JOURNAL

Pervading Emotion

....

....

....

Where in your body do you feel it?

....

....

....

Colour of Emotion

....

....

....

Shape of Emotion

....

....

....

Texture of Emotion

....

....

....

*Make the person you are with feel like the
most important person in the world.*

Pat Divilly

JOURNAL

JOURNAL

....

....

....

....

....

....

....

....

....

....

....

....

....

....

....

....

....

....

JOURNAL

Pervading Emotion

....

....

....

Where in your body do you feel it?

....

....

....

Colour of Emotion

....

....

....

Shape of Emotion

....

....

....

Texture of Emotion

....

....

....

*Give up needing to be patient and instead
live fully in the present moment.*

Mira Kelley

JOURNAL

JOURNAL

JOURNAL

Pervading Emotion

....

....

....

Where in your body do you feel it?

....

....

....

Colour of Emotion

....

....

....

Shape of Emotion

....

....

....

Texture of Emotion

....

....

....

*I do believe that the single most important thing I could ever share with you
with regard to maximising the health, harmony and happiness in your life
can be summed up in just two words: 'Love Yourself'.*

© Mike Dooley, www.tut.com

JOURNAL

JOURNAL

MEDITATION

When working on your mandala, bring awareness as often as you can to the way in which you speak to yourself. Are you berating yourself if you make a mistake or go outside a line? How we speak to ourselves during this small activity will reflect how we speak to ourselves in the bigger areas of our lives. Bringing awareness to self-talk means that we can increase self-compassion. Try not to say things to yourself that you would not be happy saying to someone else. Become your own best friend.

JOURNAL

Pervading Emotion

....

....

....

Where in your body do you feel it?

....

....

....

Colour of Emotion

....

....

....

Shape of Emotion

....

....

....

Texture of Emotion

....

....

....

Creativity is intelligence having fun.

Albert Einstein

JOURNAL

JOURNAL

JOURNAL

Pervading Emotion

....

....

....

Where in your body do you feel it?

....

....

....

Colour of Emotion

....

....

....

Shape of Emotion

....

....

....

Texture of Emotion

....

....

....

What you get by achieving your goals is not as important as
what you become by achieving your goals.

Henry David Thoreau

JOURNAL

....

....

....

....

....

....

....

....

....

....

....

....

....

....

....

....

....

....

JOURNAL

JOURNAL

Pervading Emotion

....

....

....

Where in your body do you feel it?

....

....

....

Colour of Emotion

....

....

....

Shape of Emotion

....

....

....

Texture of Emotion

....

....

....

You cannot save people, you can just love them.

Anaïs Nin

JOURNAL

....

....

....

....

....

....

....

....

....

....

....

....

....

....

....

....

....

....

JOURNAL

JOURNAL

Pervading Emotion

....

....

....

Where in your body do you feel it?

....

....

....

Colour of Emotion

....

....

....

Shape of Emotion

....

....

....

Texture of Emotion

....

....

....

If you want to view paradise,
simply look around and view it.

from *Willy Wonka & the Chocolate Factory*

JOURNAL

JOURNAL

MEDITATION

Sit comfortably in your chair with your back straight and your feet on the floor. Gaze at the mandala, bringing awareness to your breath. Notice how the chair holds you perfectly and safely.

JOURNAL

Pervading Emotion

....

....

....

Where in your body do you feel it?

....

....

....

Colour of Emotion

....

....

....

Shape of Emotion

....

....

....

Texture of Emotion

....

....

....

Maybe the journey isn't so much about becoming anything.
Maybe it's about unbecoming everything that isn't you
so you can be who you were meant to be in the first place.

Unknown

JOURNAL

JOURNAL

....

....

....

....

....

....

....

....

....

....

....

....

....

....

....

....

....

JOURNAL

Pervading Emotion

....

....

....

Where in your body do you feel it?

....

....

....

Colour of Emotion

....

....

....

Shape of Emotion

....

....

....

Texture of Emotion

....

....

....

Between stimulus and response there is a space.
In that space is our power to choose our response.
In our response lies our growth and our freedom.

Viktor E. Frankl, *Man's Search for Meaning*

JOURNAL

JOURNAL

JOURNAL

Pervading Emotion

....

....

....

Where in your body do you feel it?

....

....

....

Colour of Emotion

....

....

....

Shape of Emotion

....

....

....

Texture of Emotion

....

....

....

*Regardless of your current position in life
you are in a position to help others.*

Pat Divilly

JOURNAL

JOURNAL

JOURNAL

Pervading Emotion

....

....

....

Where in your body do you feel it?

....

....

....

Colour of Emotion

....

....

....

Shape of Emotion

....

....

....

Texture of Emotion

....

....

....

Start by doing what's necessary; then do what's possible;
and suddenly you are doing the impossible.

Francis of Assisi

JOURNAL

JOURNAL

MEDITATION

Sit comfortably, preferably in a room with no distractions. For five minutes simply gaze at the mandala. Allow and accept that these five minutes are yours alone with nothing else that you have to do but be.

JOURNAL

Pervading Emotion

....

....

....

Where in your body do you feel it?

....

....

....

Colour of Emotion

....

....

....

Shape of Emotion

....

....

....

Texture of Emotion

....

....

....

Nothing is impossible, the word itself says 'I'm possible!'

Audrey Hepburn

JOURNAL

JOURNAL

....

....

....

....

....

....

....

....

....

....

....

....

....

....

....

....

....

....

JOURNAL

Pervading Emotion

....

....

....

Where in your body do you feel it?

....

....

....

Colour of Emotion

....

....

....

Shape of Emotion

....

....

....

Texture of Emotion

....

....

....

Your work is going to fill a large part of your life, and the only way to be truly satisfied is to do what you believe is great work. And the only way to do great work is to love what you do. If you haven't found it yet, keep looking. Don't settle. As with all matters of the heart, you'll know when you find it.

Steve Jobs

JOURNAL

JOURNAL

JOURNAL

Pervading Emotion

....

....

....

Where in your body do you feel it?

....

....

....

Colour of Emotion

....

....

....

Shape of Emotion

....

....

....

Texture of Emotion

....

....

....

We must let go of the life we have planned,
so as to accept the one that is waiting for us.

Joseph Campbell

JOURNAL

....

....

....

....

....

....

....

....

....

....

....

....

....

....

....

....

....

....

....

JOURNAL

....

....

....

....

....

....

....

....

....

....

....

....

....

....

....

....

....

....

MEDITATION

Gaze at the mandala. As thoughts come to you, recognise that they are simply thoughts. Accept the thoughts, good or bad. Realise that you do not have to believe them or react to them if you choose not to.

JOURNAL

Pervading Emotion

....

....

....

Where in your body do you feel it?

....

....

....

Colour of Emotion

....

....

....

Shape of Emotion

....

....

....

Texture of Emotion

....

....

....

When you arise in the morning, think of what a precious privilege
it is to be alive – to breathe, to think, to enjoy, to love.

Marcus Aurelius

JOURNAL

JOURNAL

JOURNAL

Pervading Emotion

....

....

....

Where in your body do you feel it?

....

....

....

Colour of Emotion

....

....

....

Shape of Emotion

....

....

....

Texture of Emotion

....

....

....

The only way to make sense out of change is to plunge
into it, move with it, and join the dance.

Alan Watts

JOURNAL

JOURNAL

JOURNAL

Pervading Emotion

....

....

....

Where in your body do you feel it?

....

....

....

Colour of Emotion

....

....

....

Shape of Emotion

....

....

....

Texture of Emotion

....

....

....

If we did all the things we are capable of,
we would literally astound ourselves.

Thomas A. Edison

JOURNAL

JOURNAL

JOURNAL

Pervading Emotion

....

....

....

Where in your body do you feel it?

....

....

....

Colour of Emotion

....

....

....

Shape of Emotion

....

....

....

Texture of Emotion

....

....

....

*Mindfulness is about love and loving life. When you cultivate this love,
it gives you clarity and compassion for life, and your actions happen
in accordance with that.*

Jon Kabat-Zinn

JOURNAL

JOURNAL

....

....

....

....

....

....

....

....

....

....

....

....

....

....

....

....

....

....

MEDITATION

Gaze at the mandala. Set the intention that for the next 24 hours you will try to mindfully taste each piece of food that you put in your mouth. Savour with awareness the taste and texture of each mouthful with gratitude.

JOURNAL

Pervading Emotion

....

....

....

Where in your body do you feel it?

....

....

....

Colour of Emotion

....

....

....

Shape of Emotion

....

....

....

Texture of Emotion

....

....

....

You are never too old to set another goal or to dream a new dream.

C. S. Lewis

JOURNAL

....

....

....

....

....

....

....

....

....

....

....

....

....

....

....

....

....

....

JOURNAL

....

....

....

....

....

....

....

....

....

....

....

....

....

....

....

....

....

....

JOURNAL

Pervading Emotion

....

....

....

Where in your body do you feel it?

....

....

....

Colour of Emotion

....

....

....

Shape of Emotion

....

....

....

Texture of Emotion

....

....

....

The more tranquil a man becomes, the greater is his success,
his influence, his power for good. Calmness of mind
is one of the beautiful jewels of wisdom.

James Allen

JOURNAL

....

....

....

....

....

....

....

....

....

....

....

....

....

....

....

....

....

....

JOURNAL

....

....

....

....

....

....

....

....

....

....

....

....

....

....

....

....

....

....

JOURNAL

Pervading Emotion

....

....

....

Where in your body do you feel it?

....

....

....

Colour of Emotion

....

....

....

Shape of Emotion

....

....

....

Texture of Emotion

....

....

....

Keep love in your heart. A life without it is like
a sunless garden when the flowers are dead.

Oscar Wilde

JOURNAL

JOURNAL

JOURNAL

Pervading Emotion

....

....

....

Where in your body do you feel it?

....

....

....

Colour of Emotion

....

....

....

Shape of Emotion

....

....

....

Texture of Emotion

....

....

....

Follow your bliss and the universe will open doors where there were only walls.

Joseph Campbell

JOURNAL

....

....

....

....

....

....

....

....

....

....

....

....

....

....

....

....

....

JOURNAL

··

··

··

··

··

··

··

··

··

··

··

··

··

··

··

··

··

··

MEDITATION

*P*romise yourself to look at the sky more often!

JOURNAL

Pervading Emotion

....

....

....

Where in your body do you feel it?

....

....

....

Colour of Emotion

....

....

....

Shape of Emotion

....

....

....

Texture of Emotion

....

....

....

Progress is impossible without change, and those who cannot change their minds cannot change anything.

George Bernard Shaw

JOURNAL

JOURNAL

JOURNAL

Pervading Emotion

....

....

....

Where in your body do you feel it?

....

....

....

Colour of Emotion

....

....

....

Shape of Emotion

....

....

....

Texture of Emotion

....

....

....

*Gratitude is not only the greatest of virtues,
but the parent of all the others.*

Marcus Tullius Cicero

JOURNAL

....
....
....
....
....
....
....
....
....
....
....
....
....
....
....
....
....
....

JOURNAL

....

....

....

....

....

....

....

....

....

....

....

....

....

....

....

....

....

....

JOURNAL

Pervading Emotion

....

....

....

Where in your body do you feel it?

....

....

....

Colour of Emotion

....

....

....

Shape of Emotion

....

....

....

Texture of Emotion

....

....

....

You have power over your mind – not outside events.
Realise this, and you will find strength.

Marcus Aurelius

JOURNAL

JOURNAL

JOURNAL

Pervading Emotion

....

....

....

Where in your body do you feel it?

....

....

....

Colour of Emotion

....

....

....

Shape of Emotion

....

....

....

Texture of Emotion

....

....

....

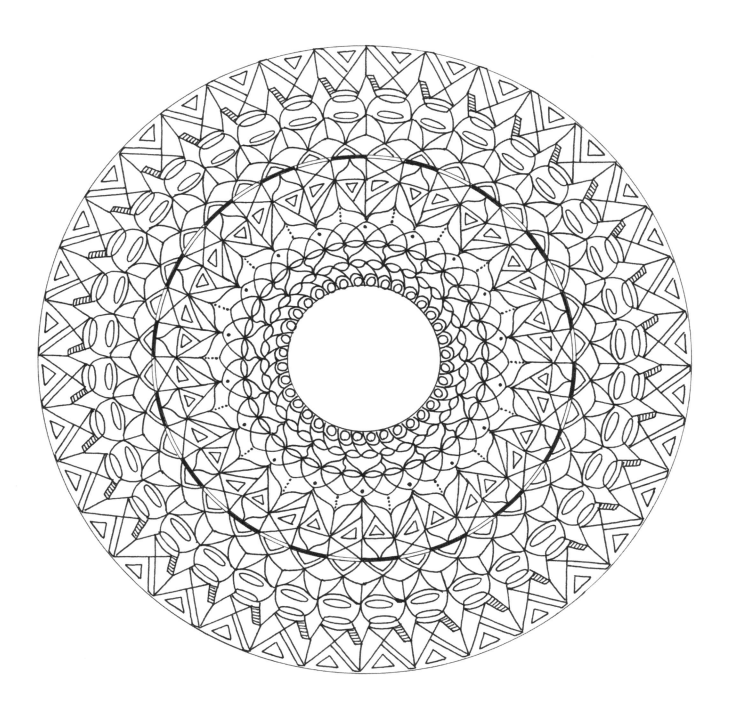

Don't forget to love yourself.

Søren Kierkegaard

JOURNAL

JOURNAL

FIRST PUBLISHED IN 2016 by
The Collins Press
West Link Park
Doughcloyne
Wilton
Cork
T12 N5EF
Ireland

A CIP record for this book is available from the British Library.

Hardback ISBN: 978-1-84889-284-2

Design and typesetting by Burns Design
Typeset in Walbaum
Printed in Malta by Gutenberg Press Limited